Life A

MW00529830

Carrie

Life According
to
Carrie

*The publisher's profits will be donated to
menetal health organizations.*

business@knightsbridgepublishing.com

ISBN: 978-1-998847-02-0

The quotations included in this book have been gathered
via multiple digital sources and researched for
authenticity and accuracy. Some
quotes collected are being presented without
context, and may therefore be imperfectly worded or attributed.
To the subject and original sources, our thanks, and where
appropriate, our apologies. – The Editor

Printed in the United States of America & United Kingdom

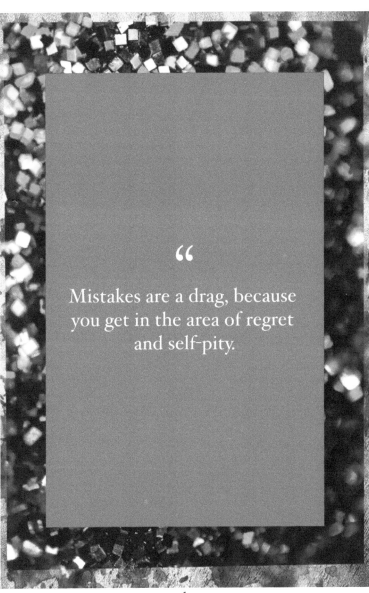

"

Mistakes are a drag, because
you get in the area of regret
and self-pity.

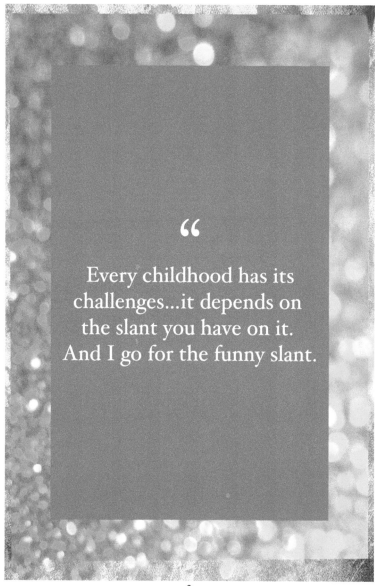

"

Every childhood has its
challenges...it depends on
the slant you have on it.
And I go for the funny slant.

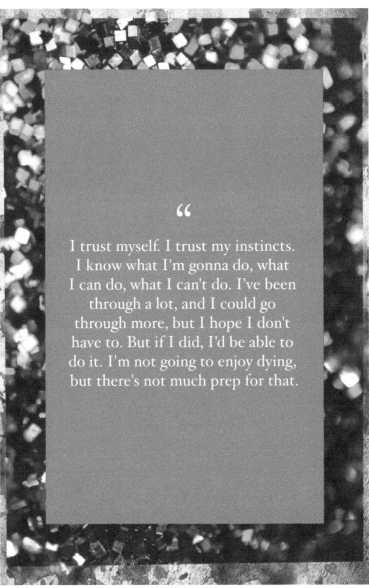

"

I trust myself. I trust my instincts.
I know what I'm gonna do, what
I can do, what I can't do. I've been
through a lot, and I could go
through more, but I hope I don't
have to. But if I did, I'd be able to
do it. I'm not going to enjoy dying,
but there's not much prep for that.

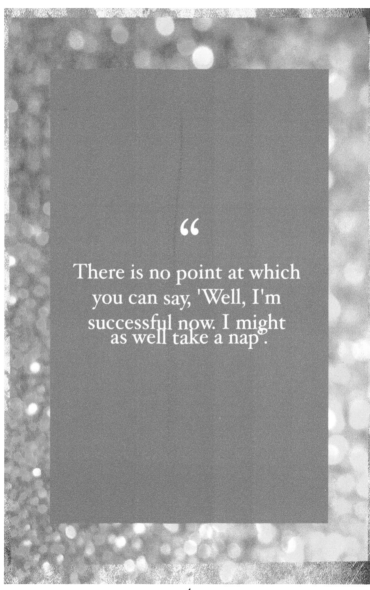

"

There is no point at which you can say, 'Well, I'm successful now. I might as well take a nap".

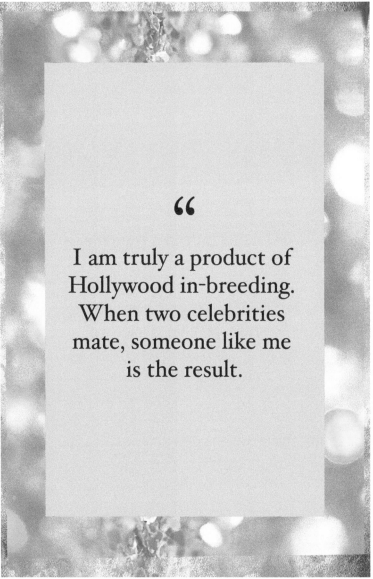

"

I am truly a product of
Hollywood in-breeding.
When two celebrities
mate, someone like me
is the result.

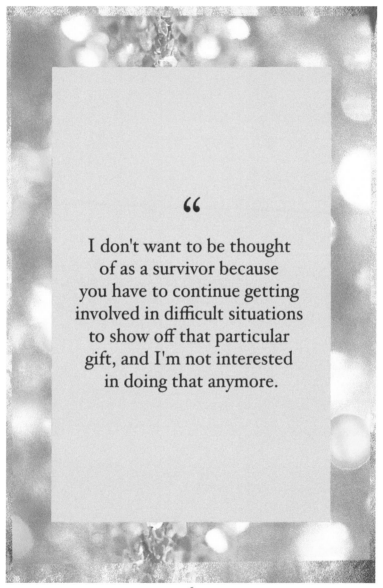

"

I don't want to be thought
of as a survivor because
you have to continue getting
involved in difficult situations
to show off that particular
gift, and I'm not interested
in doing that anymore.

"

Stay afraid, but do it anyway.
What's important is the action.
You don't have to wait to be
confident. Just do it and
eventually the confidence
will follow.

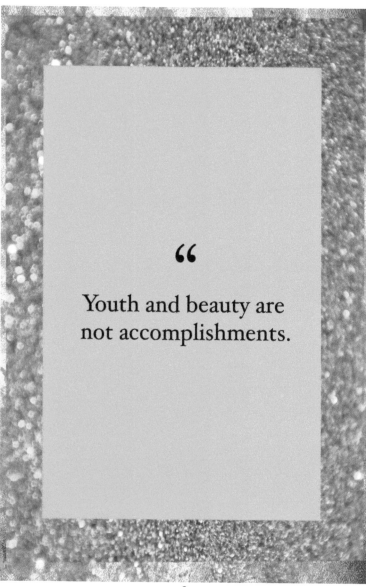

"

Youth and beauty are
not accomplishments.

"

People see me and they
squeal like tropical birds
or seals stranded on the beach.

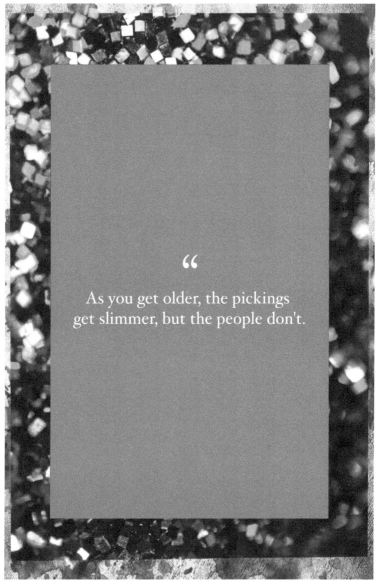

"

As you get older, the pickings
get slimmer, but the people don't.

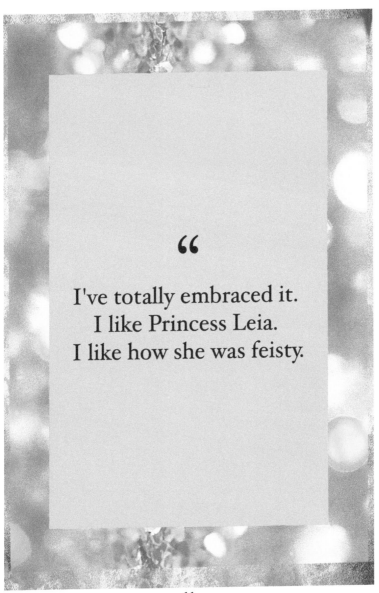

"

I've totally embraced it.
I like Princess Leia.
I like how she was feisty.

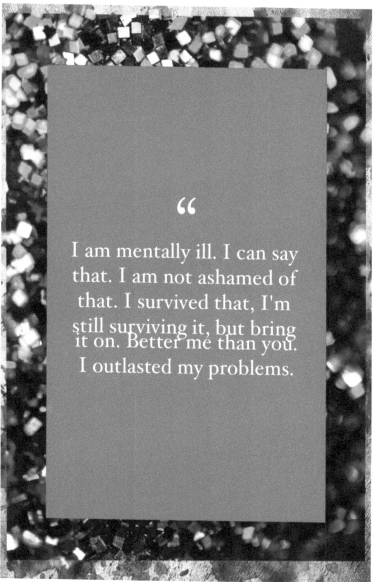

"

I am mentally ill. I can say that. I am not ashamed of that. I survived that, I'm still surviving it, but bring it on. Better me than you. I outlasted my problems.

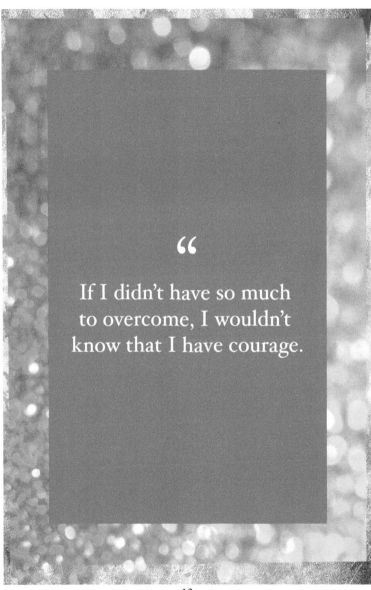

"

If I didn't have so much
to overcome, I wouldn't
know that I have courage.

"

Resentment is like drinking
poison and waiting for the
other person to die.

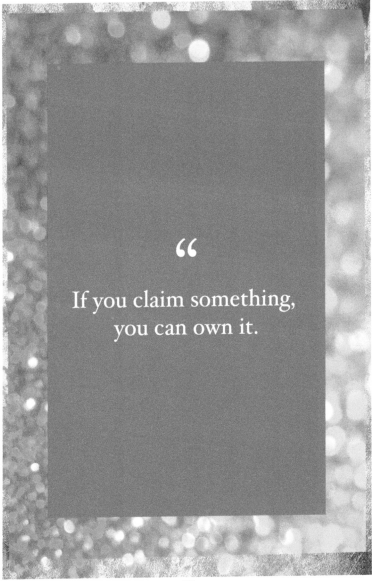

"

If you claim something,
you can own it.

"

I don't want my life to
imitate art, I want my
life to be art.

"

It creates community
when you talk about
private things.

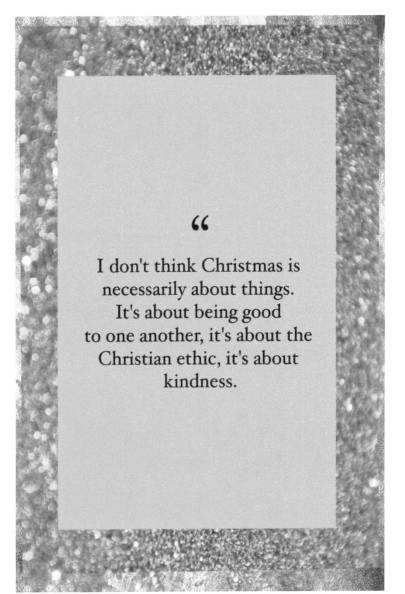

"

I don't think Christmas is
necessarily about things.
It's about being good
to one another, it's about the
Christian ethic, it's about
kindness.

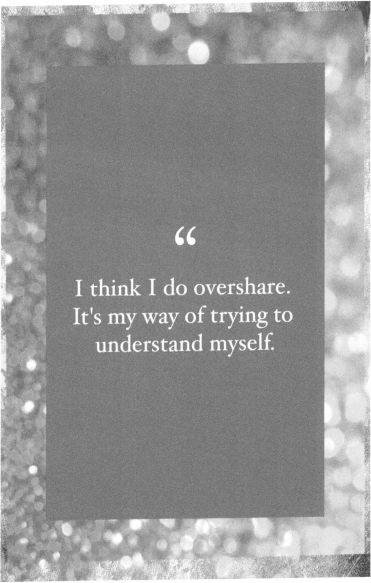

"

I think I do overshare.
It's my way of trying to
understand myself.

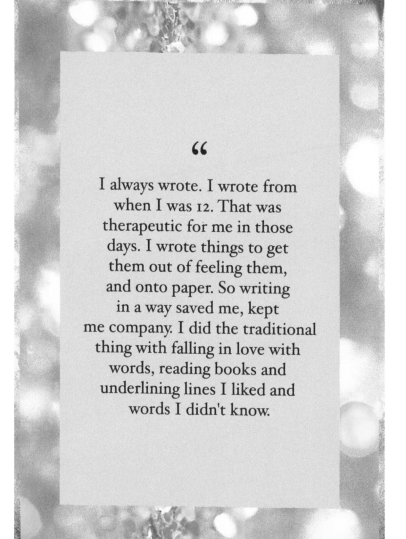

"

I always wrote. I wrote from when I was 12. That was therapeutic for me in those days. I wrote things to get them out of feeling them, and onto paper. So writing in a way saved me, kept me company. I did the traditional thing with falling in love with words, reading books and underlining lines I liked and words I didn't know.

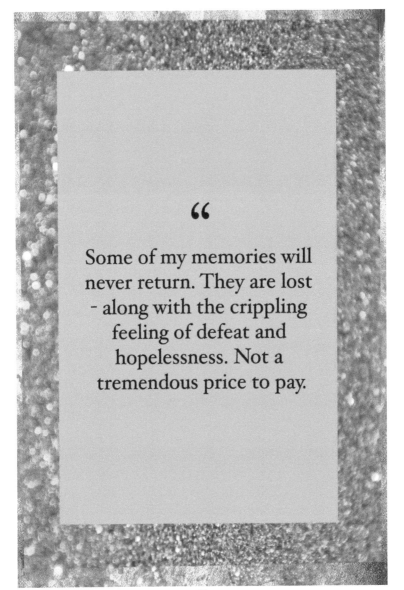

"

Some of my memories will never return. They are lost - along with the crippling feeling of defeat and hopelessness. Not a tremendous price to pay.

"

What I always wanna tell
young people now:
Pay attention.
This isn't gonna happen again.

"

I heard someone say once that
many of us only seem able to
find heaven by backing away
from hell. And while the place
that I've arrived at in my life
may not precisely be everyone's
idea of heavenly, I could swear
sometimes--I hear angels sing.

"

It's important to be able
to distinguish the difference
between a problem and
an inconvenience.

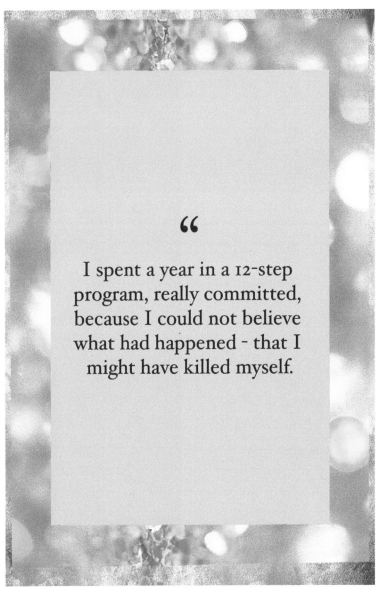

"

I spent a year in a 12-step
program, really committed,
because I could not believe
what had happened - that I
might have killed myself.

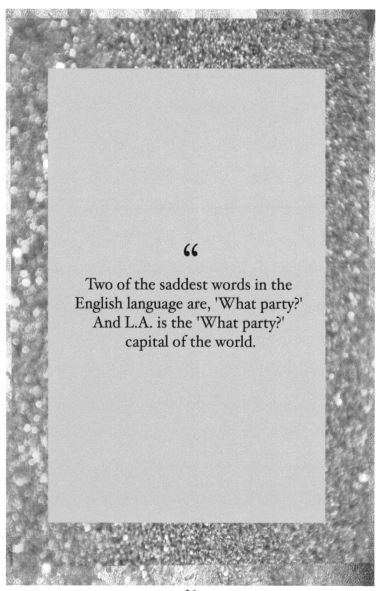

"

Two of the saddest words in the
English language are, 'What party?'
And L.A. is the 'What party?'
capital of the world.

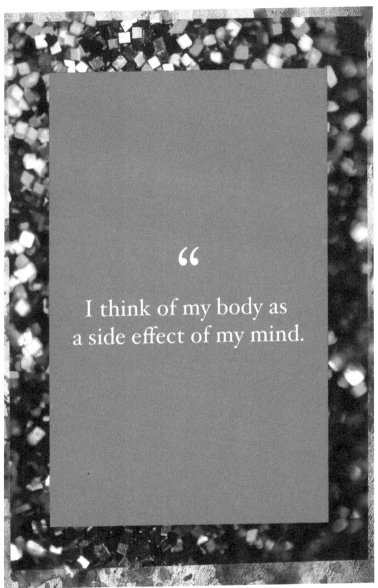

"

I think of my body as
a side effect of my mind.

"

Your innermost urges will tell you what strategy to employ to accomplish your special purpose while doing the work you enjoy.

"

You knew how humiliating
that is as an experience for
celebrities to be less of a celebrity.
There's no class to adjust to
being less famous, and you don't
think you have to worry about it.
But you do.

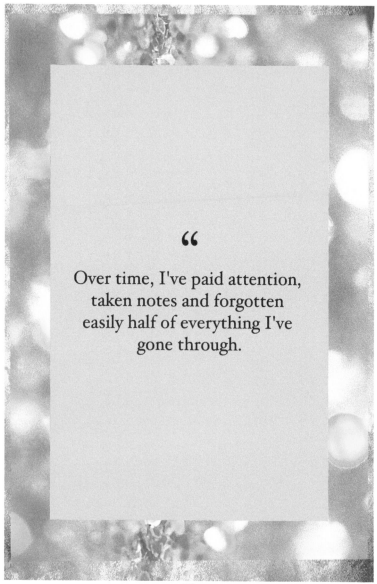

"

Over time, I've paid attention,
taken notes and forgotten
easily half of everything I've
gone through.

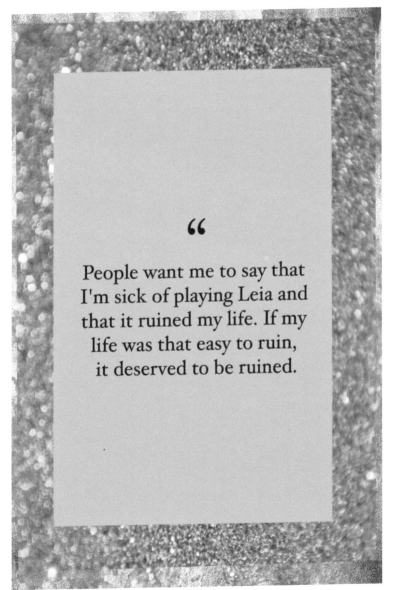

"

People want me to say that I'm sick of playing Leia and that it ruined my life. If my life was that easy to ruin, it deserved to be ruined.

"

Leia follows me
like a vague smell.

"

The older you get, the easier it is to spot the phonies.

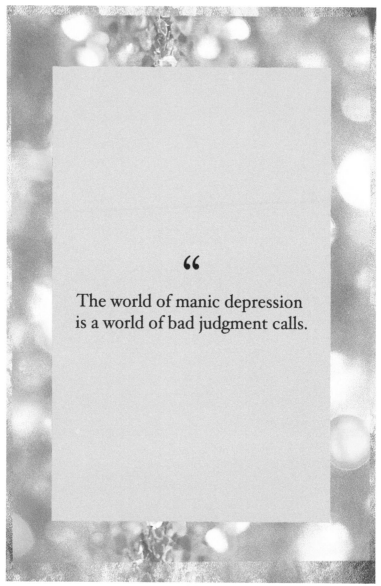

"

The world of manic depression
is a world of bad judgment calls.

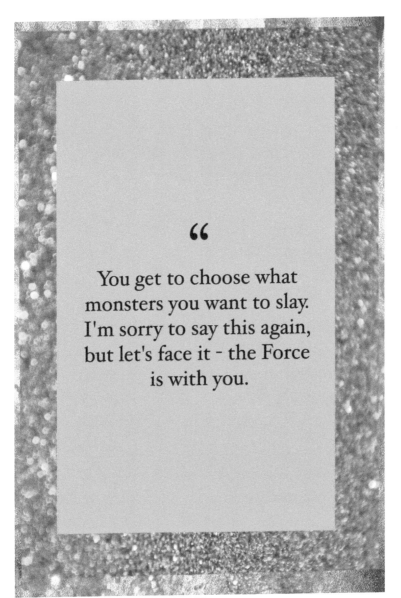

"

You get to choose what
monsters you want to slay.
I'm sorry to say this again,
but let's face it - the Force
is with you.

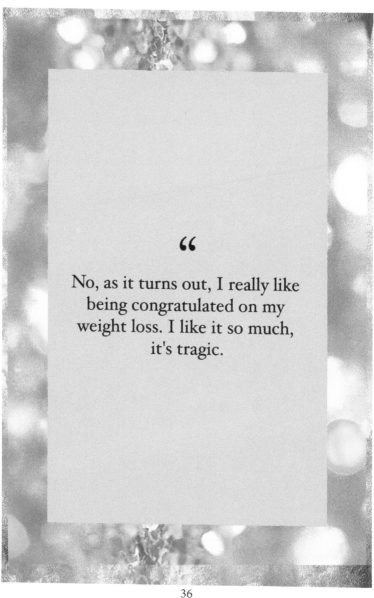

"

No, as it turns out, I really like
being congratulated on my
weight loss. I like it so much,
it's tragic.

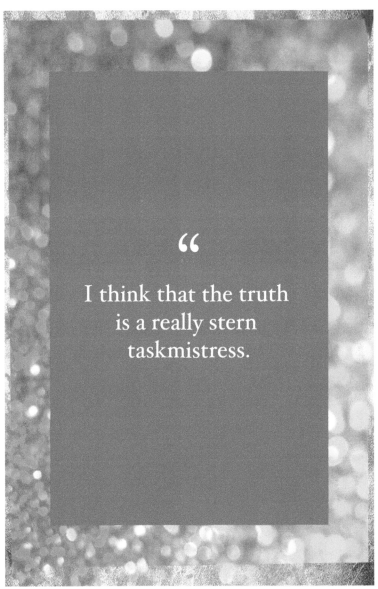

"

I think that the truth
is a really stern
taskmistress.

"

Going through challenging
things can teach you a lot,
and they also make you
appreciate the times that
aren't so challenging.

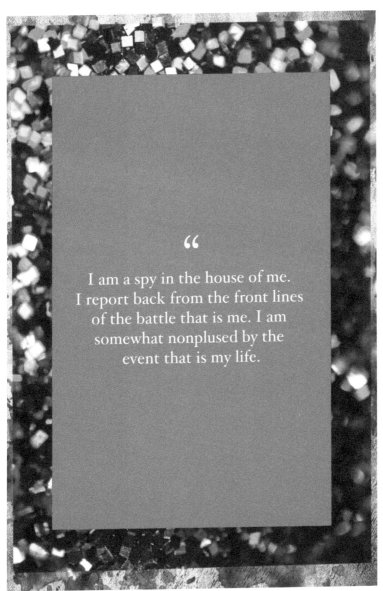

"

I am a spy in the house of me.
I report back from the front lines
of the battle that is me. I am
somewhat nonplused by the
event that is my life.

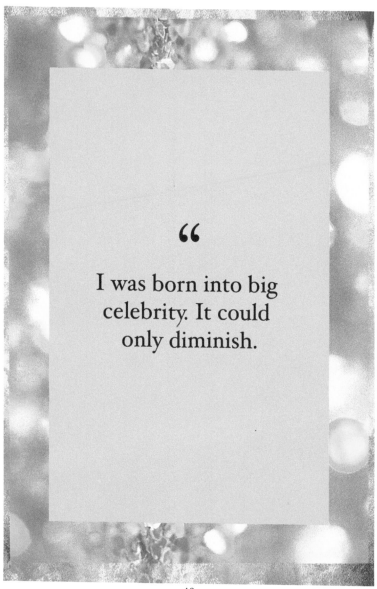

"

I was born into big
celebrity. It could
only diminish.

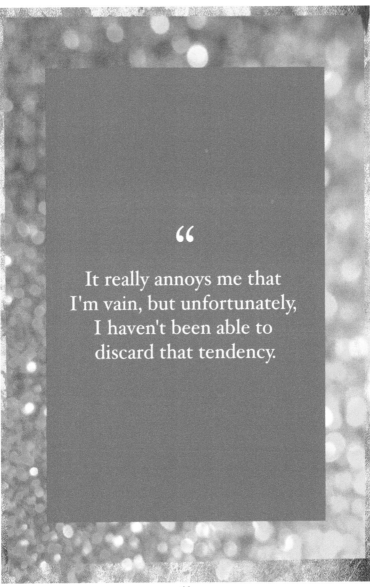

"

It really annoys me that
I'm vain, but unfortunately,
I haven't been able to
discard that tendency.

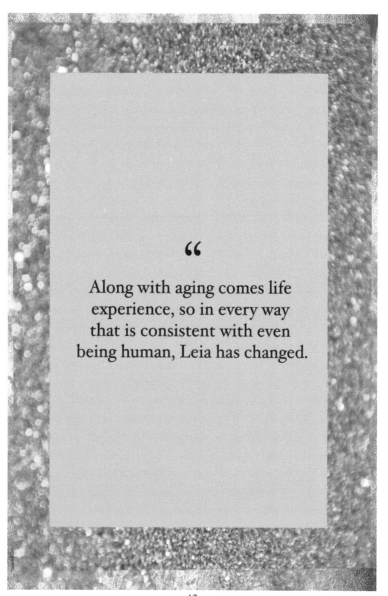

"

Along with aging comes life experience, so in every way that is consistent with even being human, Leia has changed.

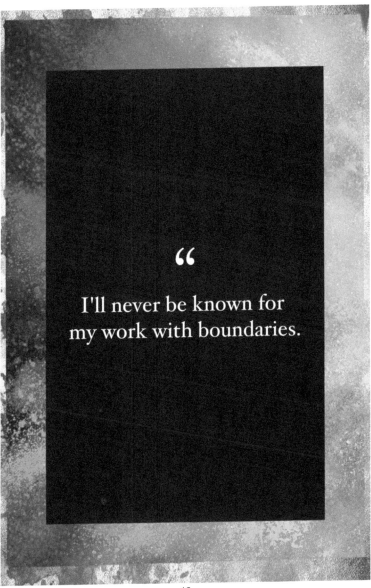

"

I'll never be known for
my work with boundaries.

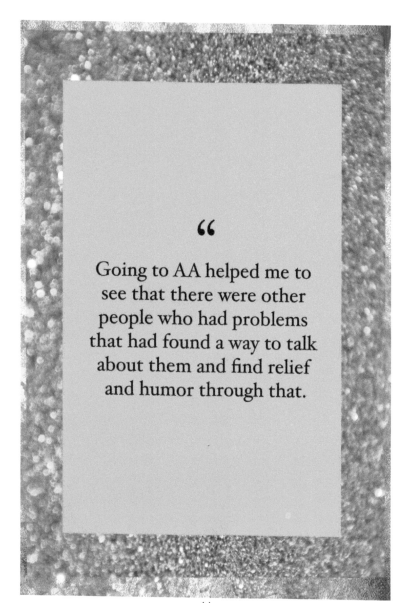

"

Going to AA helped me to
see that there were other
people who had problems
that had found a way to talk
about them and find relief
and humor through that.

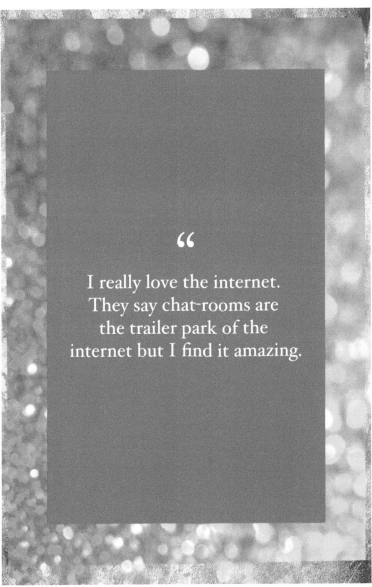

"

I really love the internet.
They say chat-rooms are
the trailer park of the
internet but I find it amazing.

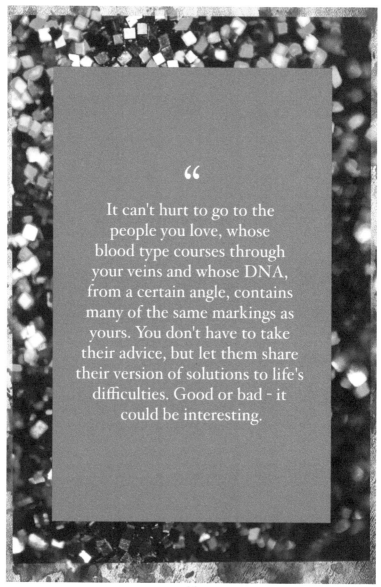

"

It can't hurt to go to the
people you love, whose
blood type courses through
your veins and whose DNA,
from a certain angle, contains
many of the same markings as
yours. You don't have to take
their advice, but let them share
their version of solutions to life's
difficulties. Good or bad - it
could be interesting.

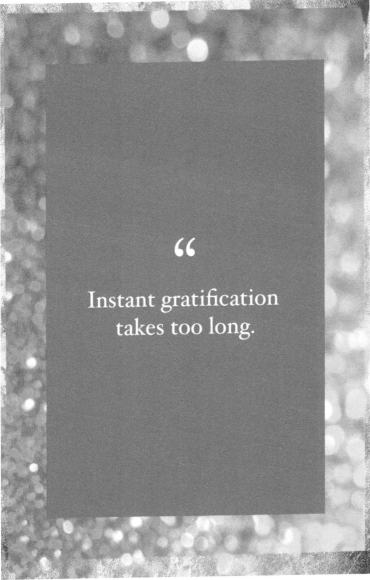

"

Instant gratification
takes too long.

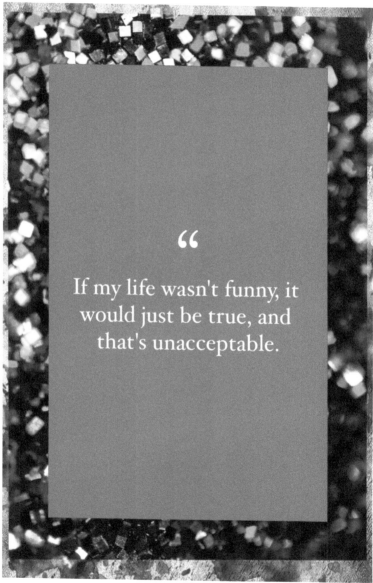

"

If my life wasn't funny, it would just be true, and that's unacceptable.

"

Females get hired along
procreative lines. After 40,
we're kind of cooked.

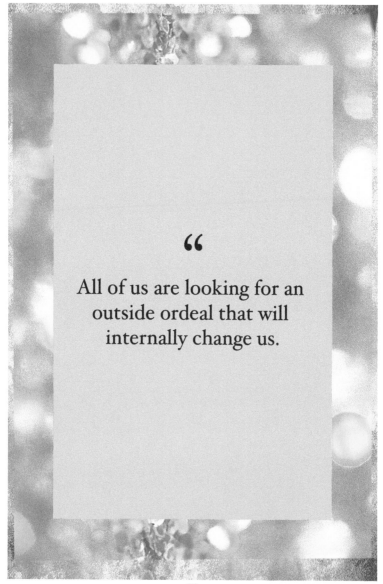

"

All of us are looking for an
outside ordeal that will
internally change us.

"

My mother's career was
over at 40 but she was
still trying to be everyone's
buddy, always smiling for
the cameras.

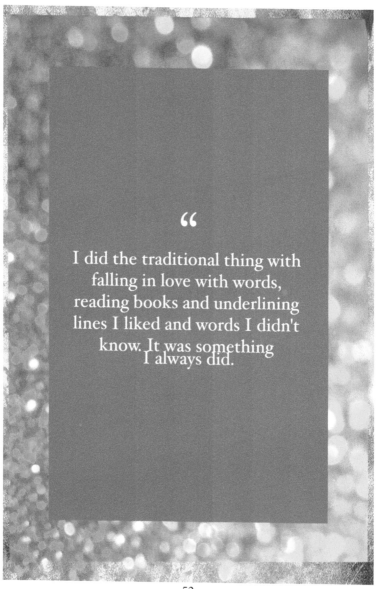

"

I did the traditional thing with
falling in love with words,
reading books and underlining
lines I liked and words I didn't
know. It was something
I always did.

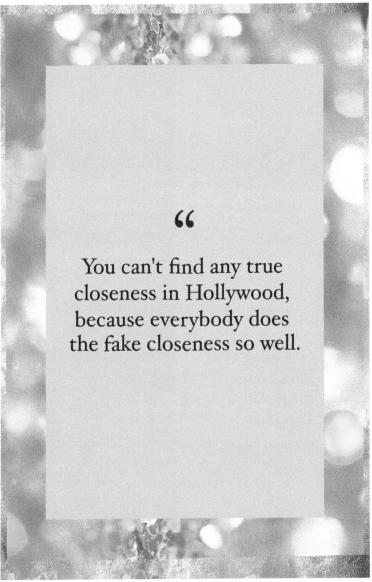

"

You can't find any true
closeness in Hollywood,
because everybody does
the fake closeness so well.

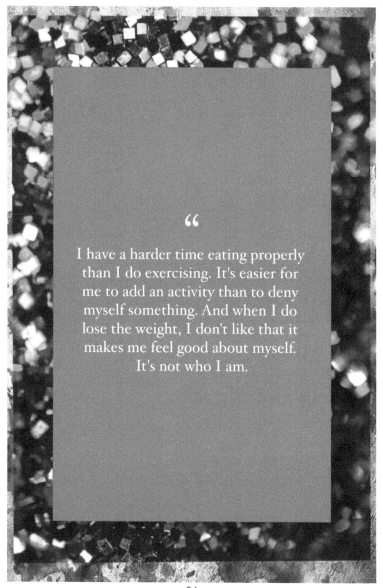

"

I have a harder time eating properly than I do exercising. It's easier for me to add an activity than to deny myself something. And when I do lose the weight, I don't like that it makes me feel good about myself. It's not who I am.

"

He's a very strange guy,
my father. I can't get mad
at him because he's so adorable.

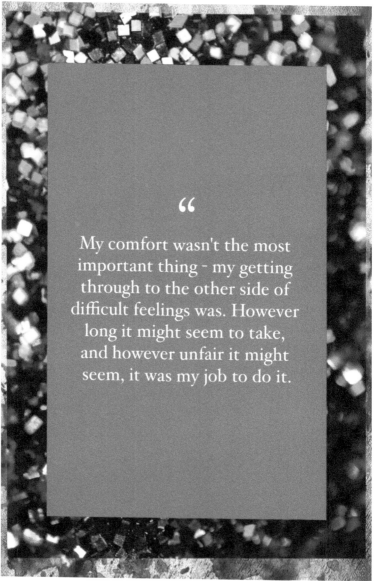

"

My comfort wasn't the most important thing - my getting through to the other side of difficult feelings was. However long it might seem to take, and however unfair it might seem, it was my job to do it.

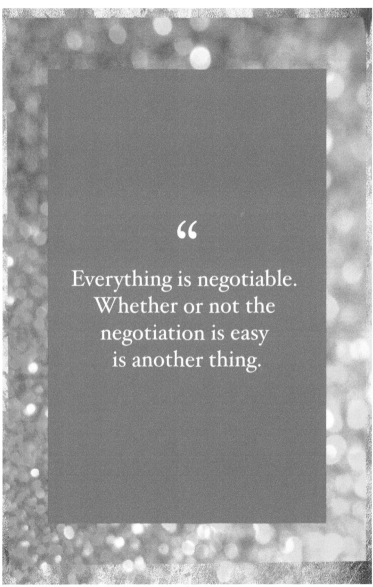

"

Everything is negotiable.
Whether or not the
negotiation is easy
is another thing.

"

I overheard people saying,
'She thinks she's so great
because she's Debbie Reynolds'
daughter!' And I didn't like it; it
made me different from other
people, and I wanted to be the same.

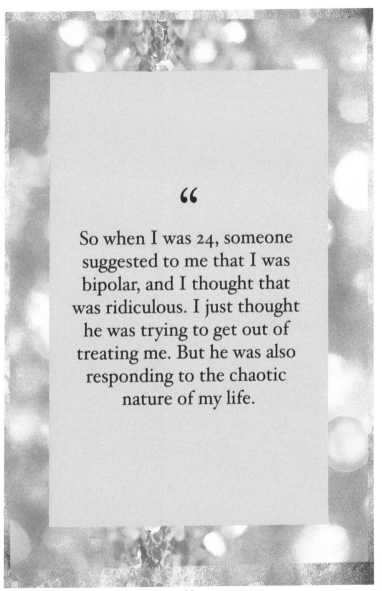

"

So when I was 24, someone
suggested to me that I was
bipolar, and I thought that
was ridiculous. I just thought
he was trying to get out of
treating me. But he was also
responding to the chaotic
nature of my life.

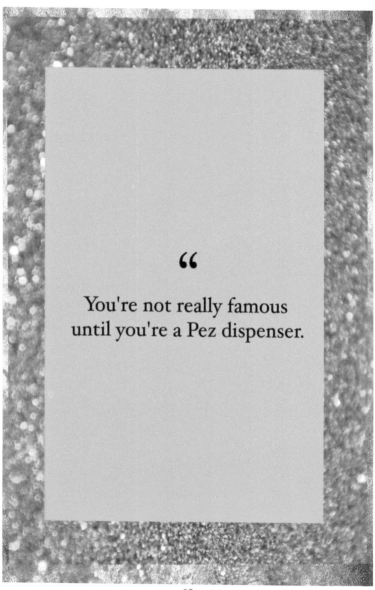

"

You're not really famous
until you're a Pez dispenser.

"

Writing is a very
calming thing for me.

"

I've seen pictures of myself
with makeup on, and I look
like those women who look
like they're wearing makeup
so they can look young, and
I don't think that's good. They
have all these products now
called - wait, what's it called,
it's my favorite - youth suppressant,
or age go away; they don't work.

Knightsbridge Publishing Group

Printed in the USA
CPSIA information can be obtained
at www.ICGtesting.com
LVHW071929031023
760054LV00020B/455

9 781998 847020